COMPILED AND EDITED BY

Jerry Rubino

An American
Christmas

16 carols and carol arrangements
from North America

MUSIC DEPARTMENT

OXFORD
UNIVERSITY PRESS

OXFORD
UNIVERSITY PRESS

Great Clarendon Street, Oxford OX2 6DP,
United Kingdom

Oxford University Press is a department of the University of Oxford.
It furthers the University's aim of excellence in research, scholarship,
and education by publishing worldwide

Oxford is a registered trade mark of Oxford University Press
in the UK and in certain other countries

Impression: 1

ISBN 978-0-19-337978-7

Music origination by
Enigma Music Production Services, Amersham, Bucks
Printed in Great Britain on acid-free paper by
Halstan & Co. Ltd, Amersham, Bucks

Preface

In 2006 I compiled and edited a choral collection of secular Christmas songs for Oxford University Press, titled *A Merry Little Christmas*. To my delight, the collection was welcomed by both critics and choirs, and I received many encouraging comments on not only the selection of songs but also the style of the arrangements. Over time, I came to realize that we had identified a sound that could be called 'American'. When I was asked to compile another choral collection for OUP, I was excited by the thought of applying the diversity of this American sound to sacred texts and well-known carols.

I was thrilled, although not surprised, by the range and quality of the compositions and arrangements that we received. In this collection you will find three original carols written by prominent American composers, arrangements of traditional carols and folk material from the US and Canada, a gospel setting of a well-known Christmas spiritual, and European carols with a jazz and Broadway twist! There is no easy way to describe the sounds created, but chord substitutions, passing dissonances, and rich, warm, melting harmonies all play their part. There are pieces with sparkle and flair, alongside startling and expansive soundscapes.

An awareness of the diversity of sound required to perform these works effectively will be vital for both choral conductor and singer. The performance practice for these styles must be considered and understood, and this includes vocal tone, articulation, dynamic contrast, pronunciation, and all the extra things that go beyond the black and white of the page. Whatever your type of choir—professional, university, concert, community, or church—get to know these works and make them your own!

It has been a pleasure to work on this collection, which brings a fresh approach to the familiar, and I hope it contributes to a festive and meaningful Christmas season across America and the rest of the world.

JERRY RUBINO
Minneapolis, Minnesota, USA

Index of Orchestrations

Contents

Performance Notes

1. Libby Larsen: A Simple Gloria

I composed 'A Simple Gloria' for the thirtieth anniversary of the University of St. Thomas Liturgical Choir (Saint Paul, Minnesota), to be sung at their annual Christmas concert. Celebrating is a joyous affair, and we often celebrate with outbursts of music teeming with fanfare, heraldry, brilliance, and boisterousness. There's another kind of celebration: a quiet, assured, and peaceful one—an 'in-burst', if you will. It's found in quiet Christmas carols like 'Silent night' and 'Lo, how a Rose e'er blooming'. 'A Simple Gloria' is a quiet Gloria. It should be sung with a hushed, serene, and reverent quality, allowing a moment of silence at the end of the music for its peaceful effect to settle.

2. Phil Mattson: Away in a manger

In my arrangement, this lovely melody and text have been set with some contemporary harmonies, which begin simply and gradually become more complex. In addition to singing it gently, as befits the words, one important key to an appropriate performance is to sing all the parts in a linear and melodic manner. Serve the carol melody, without over-emphasizing the harmonies too much or too often.

3. Randy Crenshaw: Children, go where I send thee

Like many of its kind, this traditional Appalachian 'counting song' was originally created to help children learn biblical concepts through singing and repetition. Counting songs were often performed unaccompanied, though sometimes a strummed string instrument was added. This version has an optional piano part, and hand percussion instruments can also join in. The piano part is a starting point for the accompanist, who should feel free to embellish and improvise in a rhythmic folk style, following the chord symbols provided. Many of the notes in the vocal score have a curved line in front of or after them, indicating a slide or scoop. For the most authentic performance, listen to recordings by traditional Appalachian or bluegrass vocalists, with an ear to matching their vocal tone quality and inflections.

4. Mark Sirett: D'où viens-tu, bergère?

'D'où viens-tu, bergère?' is one of the most popular lullaby carols in the francophone world. The carol takes the form of a dialogue between inquisitive villagers and a young shepherd girl who has just returned from the manger. This *a cappella* setting aims to capture the increasing curiosity that the villagers must have felt as, one by one, pieces of the miracle are revealed by the girl. The opening should capture the gentle serenity of the Christ-child, while subsequent verses depict the excited murmurings of the crowd and their changes in mood. The final verse builds to great intensity as the villagers eagerly await the reply to their final question: 'Is there nothing more?' The answer is a joyous outburst from the angelic chorus that gradually calms into the tranquility of the opening.

5. Rosephanye Powell: Go, tell it on the mountain

This arrangement of the great African-American spiritual needs a strong sense of style and enjoyment—feel free to rock throughout! The piano will add to the effect; keyboard, organ, bass, drum kit, and tambourine may also be used as additional accompaniment. The solo part at measure 11 may be sung by the alto section in lieu of a soloist, and the solo from measure 35 may be used as the basis of the singer's own improvisation, or omitted entirely.

6. Jerry Rubino: Hark! the herald-angels sing

I don't have to look at the words of this carol—they have been memorized for years. The original setting uses fairly consistent quarter-notes/crotchets for the tune, which makes it easy to remember and yet also produces goose bumps when it is sung each year. As an arranger, I wanted to create something that would maintain the traditional spirit of this carol, while engaging the singer and listener in a new way. I had to double check the meaning of 'hark!': it's a contraction from 'hearken', meaning 'listen'. My own perception is that, while the heavenly host was singing 'Gloria', the folks on the ground were responding with amazement, wonder, and joy.

I encourage you to make this a celebration of love and peace, rather than the usual up-tempo song of rushed passion. Absorb the arrangement, blending the meaning of the text with the new harmonies: use rubato and lots of expression to embrace the carol anew.

7. Sarah Quartel: Huron Carol

Inspired by the wild beauty of coastal British Columbia, this arrangement aims to invoke an atmosphere of wonder and mystery. The expansive opening of this setting reflects the vastness of the land that many Aboriginal people in Canada hold so dear and respect so deeply. The verse material offers a contrast to the opening by presenting rich harmonies with a sometimes affectionate quality, reminding the listener of the tender babe born under the moon of a harsh winter as described in Jean de Brébeuf's original text.

8. Kevin Robison: I saw three ships

One of the most enjoyable parts of my work is to take a ubiquitous tune and turn it into something new, as if it's being heard for the first time. Working with such a small amount of musical material meant that every verse had to be completely different. The arrangement seemed to benefit from a surprise ending each time, the final (where I reversed the words to 'In the morning on Christmas Day') being the biggest. The newly written lyrics building into the final bars should be carefully articulated; maintaining an understated tempo will help. Enjoy putting a new face on this peppy holiday favourite!

9. Steve Zegree: Joy to the world!

Ideal for concert, jazz, and swing choirs, this *a cappella* arrangement features fun meter changes, although the note values remain constant throughout the piece. This presents an opportunity for both conductor and singers to gain confidence with and an appreciation of changing time signatures, and keeps your listeners trying to anticipate what occurs next. Although the voice leading is relatively simple, there are a few difficult chords—you should enjoy the challenge they present to your aural skills. I suggest rehearsing these sections slowly by repeatedly moving back and forth between the changing harmonies. Have fun with the rehearsal process!

10. Mack Wilberg: Lullee, lullai, lullo, lullabye

This original carol was written for the Bach Choir of Pittsburgh with text by my friend and colleague David Warner. In the style of a lullaby carol, the piece is in verse–refrain form and should be performed in a simple yet expressive manner. It may also be effectively performed in its original version with organ accompaniment (ISBN 978-0-19-386912-7).

11. Paul Langford: O holy night!

As so many arrangements of this great Christmas classic have been written, it was a challenge and a privilege to attempt to create something new and fresh with this version. The integrity of the melody and lyrics allows for a wide range of interpretation and expression, but this arrangement is intended to reflect awe, wonder, and reverence. The piano should be flowing and expressive, but with an unwavering, steady tempo (except, of course, in the places where a ritardando is indicated). The choir should sing with a sustained and warm-bodied tone, leaning more towards the classical end of the choral spectrum. A straighter tone will allow the harmonies to truly 'lock' and tune, although a controlled, warming vibrato is welcome throughout. Observing the dynamics will also bring out the piece's full expressive potential.

12. Robert L. Jefferson: Oh, what a wonderful child

When I was a child, this piece was sung each Christmas at the church I attended. Although the song was accompanied by piano or organ, it was the rhythmic vocal parts that seemed to carry me away as I sang along. Aim to emphasize the syllable of each word, just as an instrumentalist would articulate each note. The basses should drive the piece forward, without rushing, in order to maintain a blues, laid-back feel. When you hear tapping heels and see bobbing hats in the audience, then you know you're really groovin'!

13. Bob Krogstad: On Christmas night (Sussex Carol)

This much-loved English carol has been enjoyed by listeners for many decades. In my arrangement, I have approached it as a light jazz waltz, with a playful and joyous interplay between the choir, piano, and two soloists. The divisi sections should ideally be equally weighted, especially when they appear in the three-part female voices—each part is a piece of the sonic fabric and should be balanced as such. Enjoy the breeziness of this setting, and resist the urge to make it pompous. This should be a joyful proclamation of Christ's birth!

14. Carol Barnett: Shepherds, rejoice!

With this sturdy folk carol from *The Sacred Harp* collection we celebrate the joyful aspect of the Christmas season. I have kept the straightforward feeling of the original setting and added a bit of harmonic variation through the use of canonic textures and the Lydian mode. The changing time signatures help to emphasize important words and syllables, while the refrain 'rejoice' gives us time to absorb the message of each verse.

15. Paul Johnson: Silent night

'Silent night' is one of the most beautiful of our traditional Christmas carols, with its simple, tender melody and poignant lyrics. In this new arrangement I wanted to present it in a contemporary setting so the audience feels as if they are hearing it anew. In the beginning, the vocal projection should sound more whispered than sung in full voice, and the melody starts out with the men singing unison in a lower-than-usual register to achieve this. Sing it straight, without vibrato, but aim to keep the tone warm and tender; this will also help to 'lock' the more tricky harmonies. Measures 51–7 can be sung with a more traditional sound. Most of all, focus on the lyrics and make them convincing. This is an inspired classic—an old Christmas tree with new decorations.

16. James Bassi: The blasts of chill December

The text for this carol uses the imagery and atmosphere of winter weather to convey a certain emotional and spiritual state. The darkness, the bitter winds, and the freezing snow paint a somewhat bleak picture. The triumph over this winter chill is the warmth, light, and healing of Christ the Saviour. The vivid text drew me in immediately and allowed me to explore the dynamics of this metaphor: the physical properties of weather and the spiritual struggle it represents. The tune I created, as well as the various harmonic and accompaniment textures, is meant to reflect both folk and historic church music traditions, presented within a more contemporary idiom.

Commissioned by the University of St. Thomas Liturgical Choir,
St. Paul, Minnesota, in celebration of its 30th Anniversary 1977–2007,
Robert Strusinski, conductor

1. A Simple Gloria

M. K. Dean
(b. 1950)

LIBBY LARSEN
(b. 1950)

Serene, clear ♩ = 76

And it was in a sim-ple Glo - ri - a___ that qui - et morn,

And it was in a sim-ple Glo - ri - a___ the Child was born.___

Glo - ri - a___

The an-gels sang a sim-ple Glo - ri - a___ that e-choed gent-ly through the

stars.

poco a poco accel. e cresc.

Glo - ri - a, glo - ri - a,

The shep-herds heard the sim-ple Glo - ri - a, glo - ri - a,

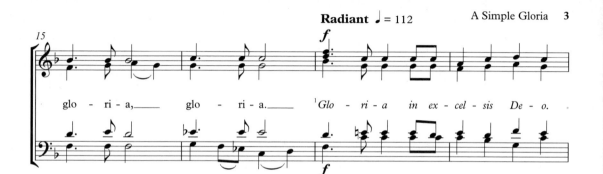

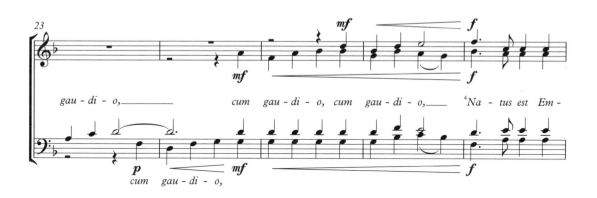

[1]Glory to God in the highest.   [2]The Saviour of the world is born.   [3]Now, with joy,   [4]Emmanuel is born.

2. Away in a manger

19th-cent. American

Melody by W. J. KIRKPATRICK (1838–1921)
arr. PHIL MATTSON (b. 1938)

The cat-tle are_ low-ing, the_ ba-by a - wakes, But_ lit-tle Lord

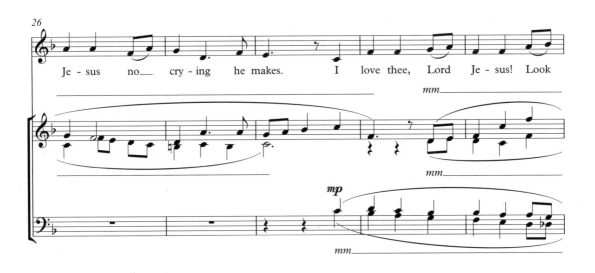

Je - sus no_ cry-ing he makes. I love thee, Lord Je - sus! Look

down from the sky, And stay by my side un - til_ morn-ing is nigh.

3. Children, go where I send thee

New lyrics (vv. 2–10) by RC

Trad. Appalachian
arr. RANDY CRENSHAW (b. 1955)

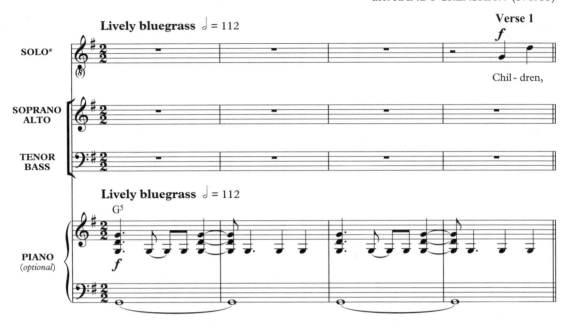

*Soprano or tenor

A tambourine or other hand percussion instrument may be played, using patterns such as the following:

See p. 19 for a separate piano part.

*pronounced 'lee'

*three, four, five, six

after v. 6 to p. 12
after v. 9 to p. 14

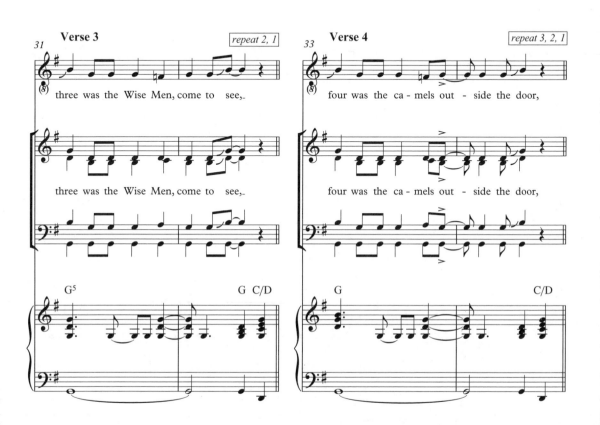

*eight, nine

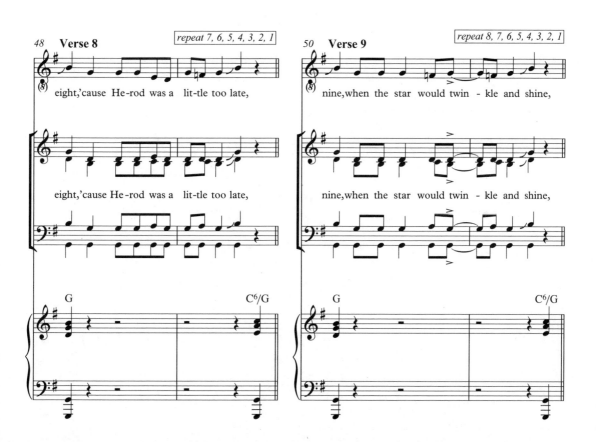

Verse 10

Chil-dren, go where I send____ thee. How will I send thee? Oh,_____

How will I send thee? Oh,_____

Oh, Law-dy,

I'm gon-na send thee ten____ by ten, ten was the pro-phets, told____ us just when,

I'm gon-na send thee ten____ by ten, ten was the pro-phets, told____ us just when,

*long, slow slide up to the note

Children, go where I send thee

(separate piano part)

Trad. Appalachian
arr. RANDY CRENSHAW (b. 1955)

to Fiona with love

4. D'où viens-tu, bergère?

trans. MS

Trad. Canadian
arr. MARK SIRETT (b. 1952)

rit.

55

Rien de____ **plus?**
Tell *us____* *more!*
ah____

rien de **plus?____** O rien de **plus?**
tell *us* *more!____* *O* *tell* *us* *more!*

rien____ de plus, ber - gè - re? Rien de plus?
tell____ *us* *more,* *dear maid - en!* *Tell* *us* *more!*

Rien____ de plus, ber - gè - re? **Rien** de plus?
Tell____ *us* *more,* *dear maid - en!* *Tell* *us* *more!*

rit.

Molto meno mosso ♩ = 92

59

Ya trois an - ges, de - scen - du____ du ciel,
Yes, *three* *an - gels,* *sing - ing from____ on high:____*

Ya trois an - ges, de - scen - du____ du ciel,
Yes, *three* *an - gels,* *sing - ing from____ on high:*

Ya trois pe - tits an - ges, de-scen-du du ciel,
Yes, there were three an - gels, *sing-ing from on high:*

Ya trois pe - tits an - ges, de-scen-du du ciel,
Yes, there were three an - gels, *sing-ing from on high:*

Molto meno mosso ♩ = 92

5. Go, tell it on the mountain

Spiritual
arr. ROSEPHANYE POWELL (b. 1962)

moun - tain that___ Je - sus Christ___ is born!

mf sing on repeat only

oo___

Go, tell it, go, tell it, go, tell it,

*Cue notes are optional pitches; *not* to be sung as a duet.

6. Hark! the herald-angels sing

Charles Wesley (1707–88)
and others

Felix Mendelssohn (1809–47)*
arr. JERRY RUBINO (b. 1952)

*Melody adapted by W. H. Cummings (1831–1915) from a chorus by Mendelssohn.

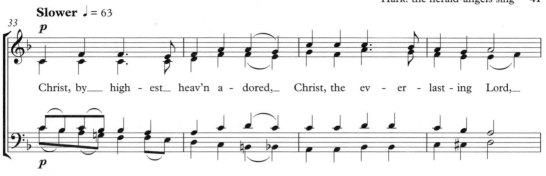

Slower ♩ = 63

p

Christ, by___ high - est heav'n a - dored,___ Christ, the ev - er - last - ing Lord,___

p

Late_ in___ time be - hold him come_ Off - spring of a vir - gin's womb:

With confidence ♩ = 80   **rit.**

*oh*_____

mp

mf

Veiled in flesh the God - head see,___ Hail th'in - car - nate De - i - ty!___

Veiled in flesh the God - head see,___ Hail th'in - car - nate De - i - ty!___

mf

mp

*oh*_____   De - i - ty!___

a tempo

mf

*Pleased as man with man to dwell, Je - sus,___ our Em - ma - nu - el.

mf

*Pleased with us in flesh to dwell,

Hark! the he - rald - an - gels sing Glo - ry__ to the new - born,

new - born.

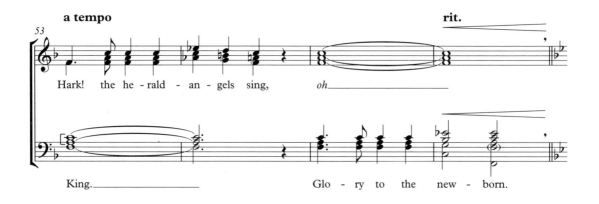

Hark! the he - rald - an - gels sing, oh_____

King._____ Glo - ry to the new - born.

Broadly ♩ = 72

Hail the heav'n born Prince of Peace!_ Hail the Sun of Right - eous - ness!

Light and life to all he brings,_ Ris'n with heal - ing in his wings;

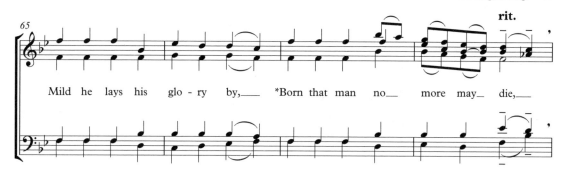

Mild he lays his glo - ry by,___ *Born that man no___ more may___ die,___

a tempo

Born to raise the sons of earth,___ Born to___ give them

se - cond birth.___ Hark! the he - rald - an - gels sing Glo - ry,

rit.

glo - ry, glo - ry___ to the new - born___ King.

*Born that we no more may die, Born to raise us from the earth, Born to give us second birth.

7. Huron Carol

St Jean de Brébeuf (*c.*1643)
trans. Jesse Edgar Middleton (1872–1960)

Trad. Canadian
arr. SARAH QUARTEL (b. 1982)

'Twas in the moon of win-ter-time when

all the birds had fled, That might-y Git-chi Man-i-tou sent

an-gel choirs in-stead; Be-fore their light the stars grew dim, and

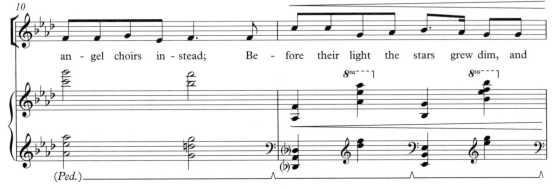

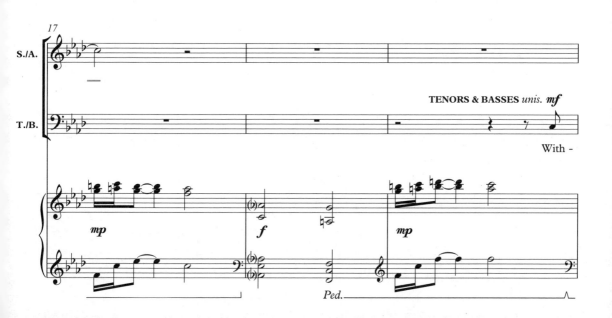

37

Je - sus is born, *in ex - cel - sis glo - ri - a.*

poco rit. *f* a tempo

40

O chil - dren of the fo - rest free, O

unis.

poco rit. a tempo

Ped. sim.

42

sons of Man - i - tou,___ The Ho - ly Child of earth and hea - ven is

8. I saw three ships

Trad. English
arr. KEVIN ROBISON (b. 1966)

Pray, whi - ther sailed those ships all

T.
B.

three? On Christ - mas Day, on Christ - mas

Day, Pray, whi - ther sailed those ships all

*Additional words by Kevin Robison.

9. Joy to the world!

Isaac Watts
(1674–1748)

LOWELL MASON (1792–1872)
based on Handel
arr. STEVE ZEGREE

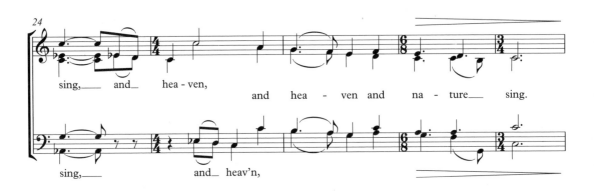

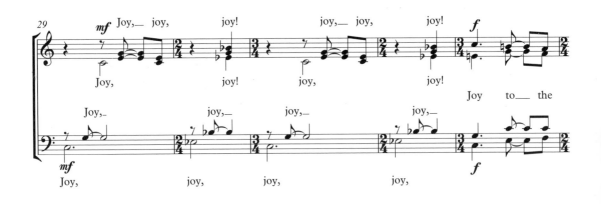

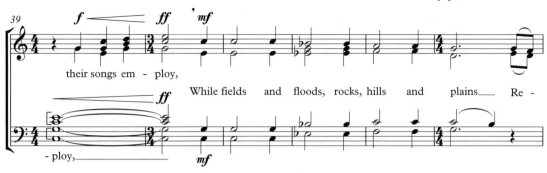

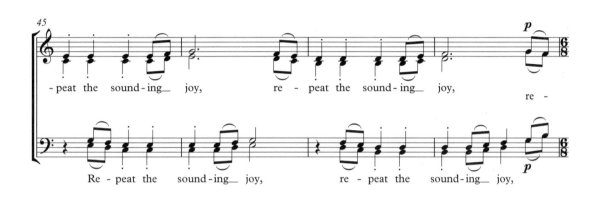

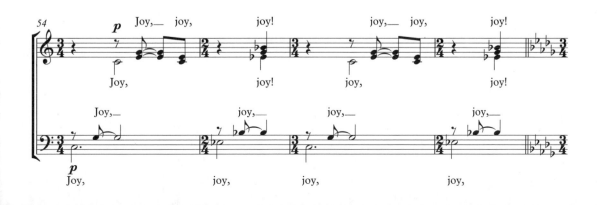

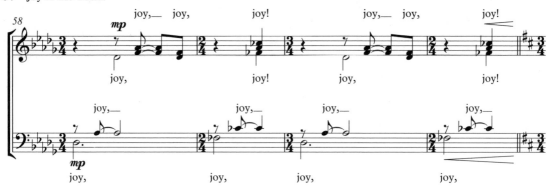

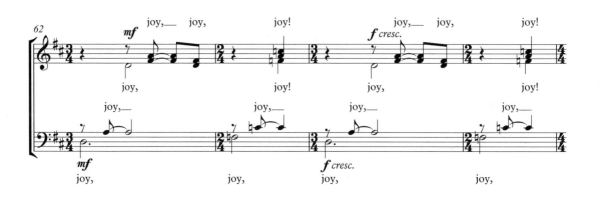

Triumphantly

He rules the world with truth and— grace, And makes the na - tions

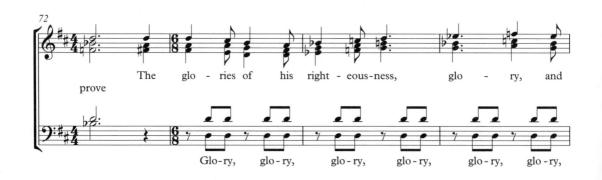

The glo - ries of his right - eous-ness, glo - ry, and

prove

Glo-ry, glo-ry, glo-ry, glo-ry, glo-ry, glo-ry,

wonders of his love,_____ and__ wonders of his love,_____ and__

wonders,_____ wonders_____ of his__ love.

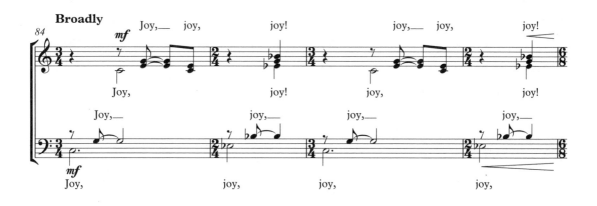

Joy,__ joy, joy! joy,__ joy, joy!
Joy, joy! joy, joy!
Joy,__ joy,__ joy,__ joy,__
Joy, joy, joy, joy,

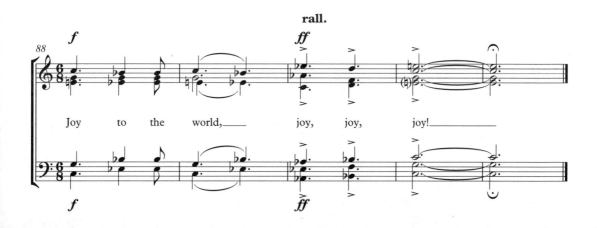

Joy to the world,_____ joy, joy, joy!_____

Commissioned by the Barlow Endowment for Music
Composition at Brigham Young University for the Bach Choir of Pittsburgh,
Brady Allred, conductor

10. Lullee, lullai, lullo, lullabye
(O who will come and listen this night?)

David Warner

MACK WILBERG
(b. 1955)

poco rit.

eyes that sure - ly will grieve For all good souls who are

blind - ed this night? Come near, be - hold, and see by His light.

poco rit.

a tempo

Lul - lee, lul - lai,* Come, ox - en, draw nigh. Lul -

*Rhyme with 'lullabye'.

-lee, lul - lai, lul - lo, lul - la - bye.

a tempo
SOPRANO

S. O who will come and won - der this hour At one bright

star held up by His pow'r To lead us all from our

wan - der-ing ways? Come close be - side the Shep - herd to stay.

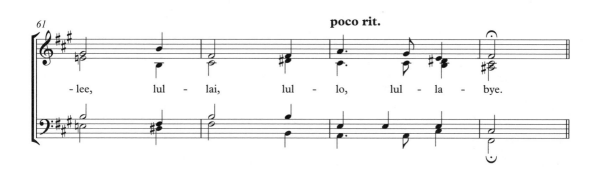

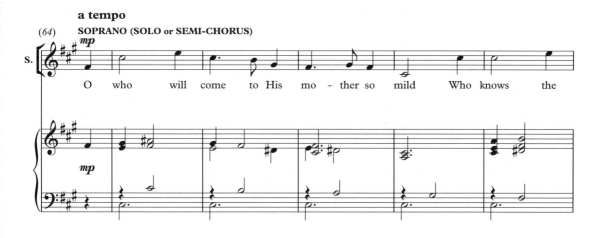

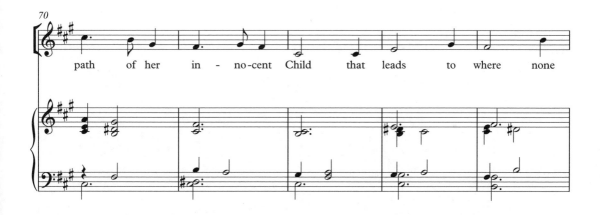

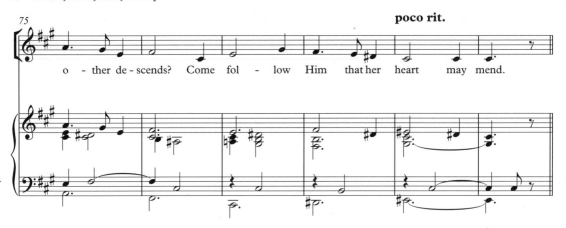

Him who suf - fers our plight, That ris - ing, we may

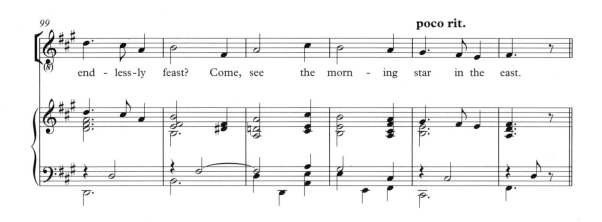

poco rit.

end - less-ly feast? Come, see the morn - ing star in the east.

a tempo

(104)

S.
A.

Lul - lee, lul - lai, Come all now draw nigh. Lul -

T.
B.

- lee, lul - lai, lul - lo, lul - la - bye.

11. O holy night!

Placide Cappeau de Roquemaure (1808–77)
trans. John S. Dwight

Adolphe Adam (1803–56)
arr. PAUL LANGFORD (b. 1966)

Fall_____ on your knees!_____ O hear_____

_____ the an - gel voi - - ces! O night_____ di-

- vine!_____ O__ night   when Christ was born!_____

12. Oh, what a wonderful child

Trad. American
arr. ROBERT L. JEFFERSON (b. 1960)

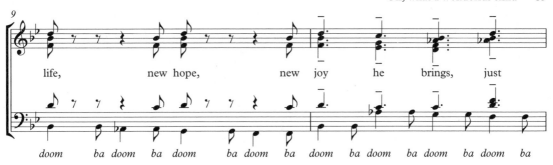

life,   new hope,   new joy he brings, just

doom ba doom ba doom ba doom ba doom ba doom ba doom ba doom ba

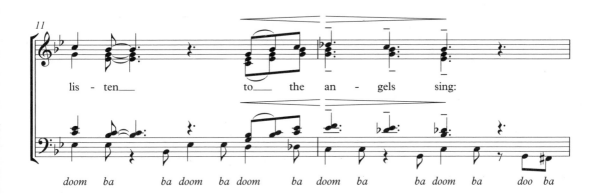

lis - ten___   to___ the an - gels sing:

doom ba   ba doom ba doom   ba doom ba   ba doom ba   doo ba

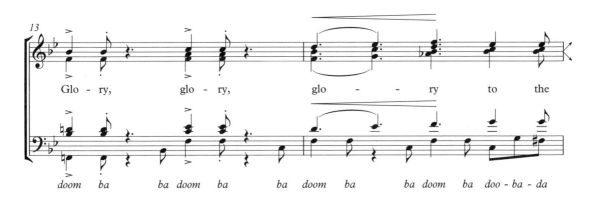

Glo - ry,   glo - ry,   glo - - ry   to the

doom ba   ba doom ba   ba doom ba   ba doom ba doo - ba - da

S. new - - born___   King!

A. new - - born___   King!

new - - born___   King!

T.
B. *doom ba doo - ba - da doom ba doo - ba - da   doom   doom ba doom ba doom ba*

*The solo can be alternated between a male and female soloist if desired, e.g. on 'Three wise men' (bar 24).
Bar 29 could be sung by both soloists together.

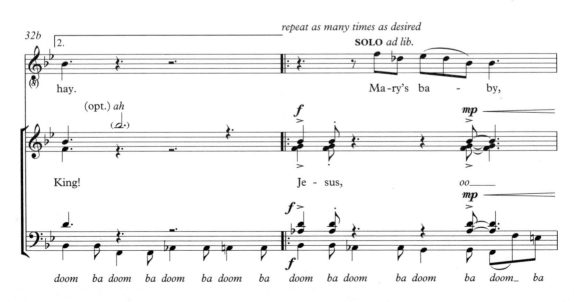

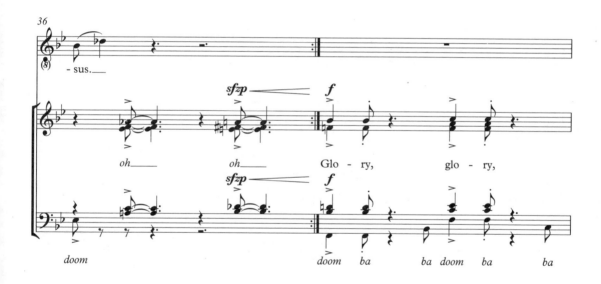

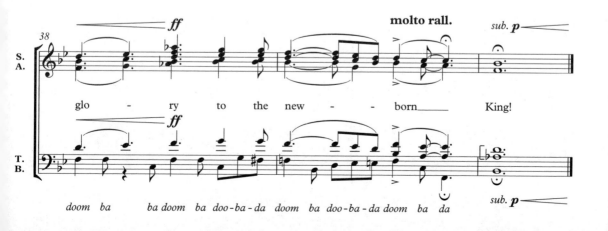

13. On Christmas night
(Sussex Carol)

Trad. English
arr. BOB KROGSTAD (b. 1950)

our mer - ci - ful King's birth.

SOLOIST 1* *mf*

Then why should men on

dt do do dt do do

earth be so sad, Since our Re - deem - er made us

dt do do dt do do dt do do dt do do dt do do

*Soprano or alto

*Tenor or bass

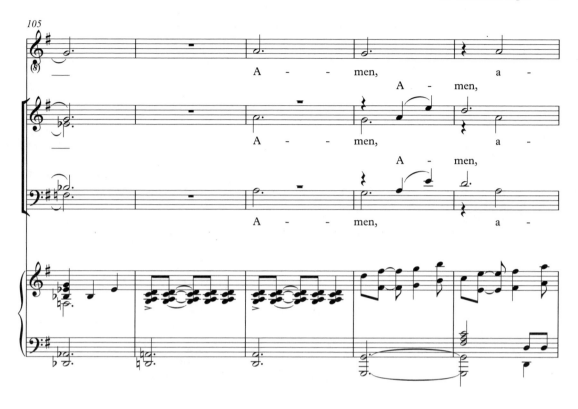

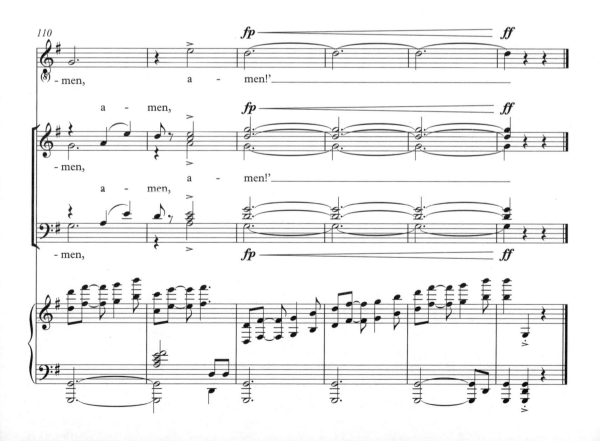

14. Shepherds, rejoice!

Isaac Watts (1674–1748)

L. P. Breedlove*
arr. CAROL BARNETT (b. 1949)

*The melody is taken from the shape-note collection *The Sacred Harp*. Breedlove flourished in South Georgia in the mid nineteenth century; his exact dates are unknown.

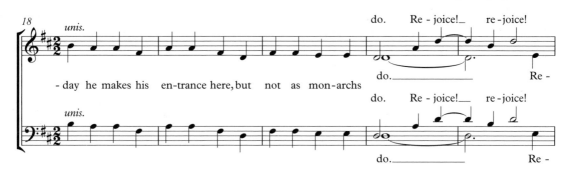

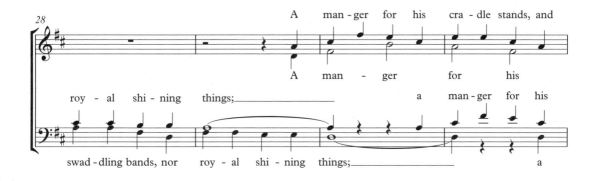

-ry to God that reigns a-bove, let peace sur-round the earth; mor-tals

__ shall know their Mak-er's love_____ at their Re - deem - er's

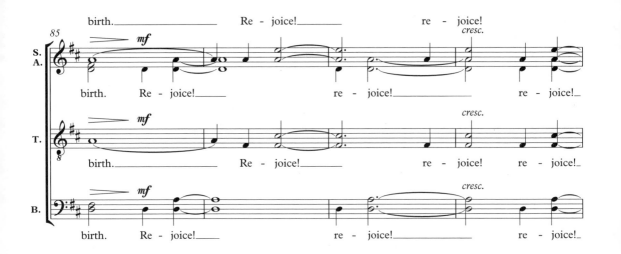

birth._____ Re - joice!_____ re - joice!

birth. Re - joice!_____ re - joice!_____ re - joice!

birth._____ Re - joice!_____ re - joice! re - joice!

birth. Re - joice!____ re - joice!_____ re - joice!

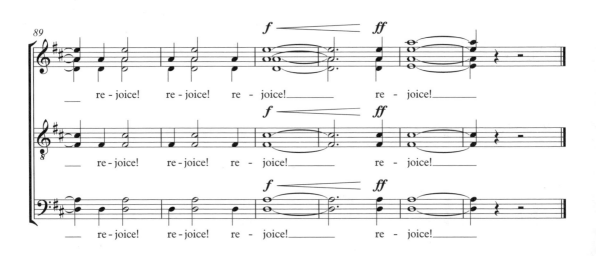

__ re - joice! re - joice! re - joice!_____ re - joice!

__ re - joice! re - joice! re - joice!_____ re - joice!

__ re - joice! re - joice! re - joice!_____ re - joice!

15. Silent night

Joseph Mohr (1792–1848)
trans. John F. Young

Franz Gruber (1787–1863)
arr. PAUL JOHNSON (b. 1946)

16. The blasts of chill December

Norval Clyne
(1817–90)

JAMES BASSI
(b. 1961)

The wel-come snow at Christ-mas-tide falls shi-ning from the skies: On vil-lage paths and up-lands wide all ho-ly-white it lies; It

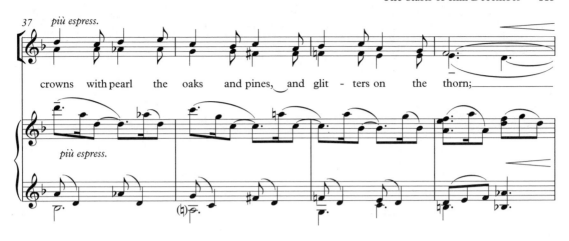

crowns with pearl the oaks and pines, and glit - ters on the thorn;

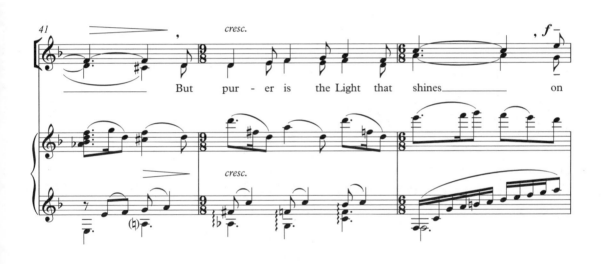

But pur - er is the Light that shines on

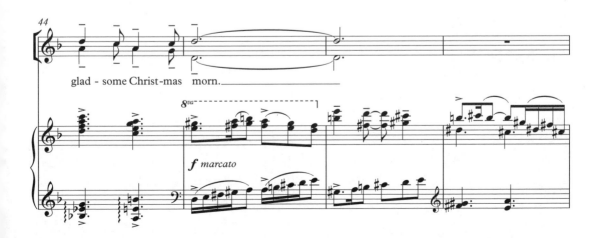

glad - some Christ-mas morn.

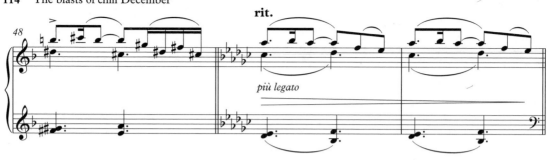

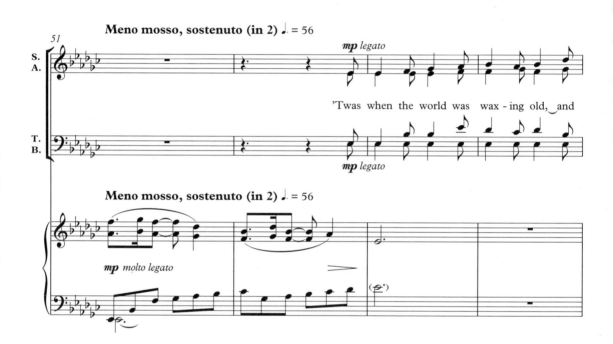

heav'ns un-fold a light be-yond the day; The

Lord of Heav'n's e - ter - nal height for us a Child was

born; And He, the ve - ry Light of